In the Beginning was Chaos

Greek Myths of the Gods and Creation

2nd Edition 2018

Sarah L. Maguire

Contents

Introduction

Creation myths are often somewhat neglected in popular retellings of Greek myths. The emphasis instead tends to be very much on the human; the quests of mighty heroes such as Herakles or Jason or events such as the great Trojan War or the downfall of great dynasties such as the House of Atreus or the Theban House of Labdacos.

Like other ancient peoples, however, the Greeks had their mythological traditions about the beginning of the world and how the first humans and the first gods and goddesses came into being and why things are as they are.

Our most important source for creation stories in Greek mythology comes from the work of the poet Hesiod. A farmer from Boeotia in Central Greece, Hesiod flourished around the seventh century BCE in what is called the Archaic period, preceding the full flowering of the Classical age. Together with Homer, Hesiod is among the earliest of the Greek authors whose work has come down to us. Hesiod composed two major poems that have survived largely intact; the *Theogony* and *Works and Days* as well as other poems surviving in more fragmentary form such as the *Catalogue of Women.*

The *Theogony* tells the story of the coming into being of the first divine entities, the creation of the world and the brutal struggle for mastery between successive generations of the Gods, culminating in the triumph of Zeus and the Olympians.

Works and Days is a didactic poem offering practical and moralising advice to the farmer. This poem, focusing more on our present condition as human beings, also introduces stories about the origins of human existence, including more stories about Prometheus, the story of Pandora the first woman, which Hesiod lends strongly misogynistic overtones, and the important myth of the Five Ages of Man, versions of which appear in many cultures from classical India to ancient Israel.

Hesiod's account of the first stories of the Gods and the world became the standard version in Greek literature, though innumerable alternative traditions co-existed, most notably in the writings of the Orphic mystery cult, which had its own distinctive mythology.

The central creation myths told to us by Hesiod and by later classical writers appear to have been strongly influenced by the stories and cultures of the Near East, in particular, Mesopotamia.

The *Enuma Elish* is an epic poem that was found largely preserved on clay tablets in the ruined library of Assurbanipal, King of Nineveh in the 7th century BCE. Written in cuneiform script, in the Old Babylonian language, the *Enuma Elish* tells the story of the creation of the world, the genesis of the gods and struggles between successive generations of gods culminating in the triumph of the God Marduk.

Like the *Enuma Elish*, Hesiod's *Theogony* tells of successive generations of deities competing ruthlessly for supreme power, with the Earth, Sea, and Sky personified as divine actors in the often-bloody drama.

While Hesiod is my primary source for the account of the birth, generation and struggles of the first deities, I have drawn upon various other ancient authors for the more detailed accounts of the Olympian deities and for many of the stories of the emergence of humanity and human culture.

The Athenian playwright Aeschylus' tragedy *Prometheus Bound* offers a vivid and passionate dramatization of the downfall of Prometheus which Hesiod sketches. The *Metamorphoses* of the Roman poet Ovid is always an invaluable and entrancing companion when researching mythology and his full account of Deucalion's flood was particularly useful here.

The so-called *Homeric Hymns*, deriving mostly from the pre-classical period, around the same time Hesiod was writing, are a vital source for tales of the individual Olympian divinities. In particular, I used the *Hymn to Demeter* and the *Hymn to Hermes*.

Apollodorus of Alexandria's *Library of Greek Mythology*, the only summary retelling of the full span of Greek mythology surviving from the ancient Greek world, remains an essential and handy resource for any Greek mythographer.

In the Very Beginning – Chaos and the First Primal Deities

Before there was anything else, Hesiod tells us, there was Chaos. Chaos was a goddess of sorts, a black, yawning void, an empty place of potential for things to happen in. We might call her Space.

In the midst of Chaos, in the very centre of that yawning void, according to ancient cosmology, Gaia the Earth came into being, seemingly spontaneously. Third came Eros, the cosmic deity of love and creation, very different from the little winged mischief beloved of Renaissance art.

From Chaos then, was engendered Erebos (Darkness), a god and Nyx (Night) a goddess. Nyx and Erebos came together in love, and the dark goddess gave birth to Aether (the upper atmosphere above the clouds) and Hemera (Day).

Gaia, by means of her own fertile power, now brought forth the Sky God Ouranos, who passionately embraced her on all sides. Gaia also brought to birth hills and mountains, rising up from her own broad body. Here the divine Nymphs would make their home. She brought into being Pontos, the great Sea, flooding much of the Earth's dry expanse.

The Children of Gaia and Ouranos

So far, Gaia had engendered her offspring by herself, but now, moved by Eros, she joined in love with Ouranos and gave birth to the generation of Titans, twelve in all, six Gods and six Goddesses.

Their names were:

Theia

Rheia

Themis (Goddess of law and custom)

Mnemosyne (Memory, Mother of the Muses)

Phoebe (a Moon Deity)

Tethys (a Sea Goddess)

Okeanos (The Ocean)

Koios

Krios

Hyperion (a Sun Deity)

Iapetos (Ancestor of Prometheus and Epimetheus)

and Kronos

Gaia next produced three more sons; the Cyclopes, whose names were Brontes (Thunderer), Steropes (Lightner), and Arges (Bright). They were strong and proud of spirit and were able smiths and craftsmen. Much later, they would forge Zeus' thunderbolt. The Cyclopes resembled their Titan siblings, who were basically human in form, but with one striking difference; they each had but one round, staring eye set in the centre of their foreheads. The name Cyclops means Round-Eye.

The three sons born to Gaia after the Cyclopes were even stranger in appearance and mightier and more terrible still. Each of them had fifty heads on his shoulders and each had a hundred arms, fifty sprouting from each giant shoulder. All three were imbued with immense strength and power. Their names were Cottos, Briareos and Gyes, known collectively as the Hekatonchaires or the Hundred-Handed.

The Sky God, Ouranos, their father, was horrified and alarmed by these strange and powerful children, so much so that he thrust the Cyclopes and the Hekatonchaires back into his wife Gaia's womb, burying them deep inside the earth that was her body, rejoicing in this neat solution to his problematic offspring.

The Downfall of Ouranos

Gaia, naturally, was angered and distressed by the forcible return of her six sons to her womb. After brooding for a time on this injustice, Gaia formed within herself a mass of grey, hard flint. She took some and fashioned it into a sharp sickle.

Calling the rest of her sons together, Gaia urged them to help her take vengeance on their father Ouranos for his cruel and outrageous act. The Titans, however, were stricken with fear at the thought of confronting their terrifying father and they greeted her words with silence. The exception was Kronos, the youngest. He spoke up and told his mother he was willing to carry out her plan as he had no respect for his evil father who had wronged the family.

Gaia rejoiced in the courage of her youngest son and showed Kronos where he was to remain concealed in ambush, armed with the sharp flint sickle.

When night fell, Ouranos approached in amorous mood. Stretching himself above his wife, the Earth, the Sky God embraced her on all sides, and as he did so, Kronos darted out from his hiding place and, with a great sweep of the iron sickle, he castrated his own father.

As the Sky God's seed poured forth in great, bloody gouts, Gaia received it. In the fullness of time, she would give birth to the three Erinyes: Alecto, Tisiphone and Megaira, the snaky-haired Furies who pursue into madness those who slay their own kin. She would also bring forth a race of warlike Giants and the Melian Nymphs, guardians of the ash trees.

The Birth of Aphrodite

Ouranos' genitals themselves were cast into the sea, where they were borne hither and thither by the waves for some time in a cloud of white foam. Within this foam, emanating from the God's severed flesh, there grew a divine maiden of unsurpassable beauty, fully formed and borne aloft on the waves.

First, the maiden approached the Island of Kythera, but it was at Paphos on the Island of Cyprus that she finally stepped ashore. As she stepped on to dry land, attended by Eros and Desire, the green grass sprouted up around her bare feet. Thus, from Kronos' ugly act was born lovely Aphrodite, Goddess of Love. The epitome of a beautiful woman of marriageable age, Aphrodite is the goddess of sexuality and desire. She is associated, of course, with the sea and with doves and sparrows. The flowering myrtle is her plant. Aphrodite is closely associated with the Sumerian goddess Ishtar.

Later accounts make Aphrodite the daughter of Zeus, placing her as subordinate to the ruling king of the Gods, but, in fact, she is of an older, more primal generation than the Olympians.

Kronos replaced his usurped father as ruler over all the Gods. Mutilated and defeated, the Sky God Ouranos warned his rebellious sons, the Titans, that because of Kronos' wicked and presumptuous action, their own bitter downfall would be upon them in time to come.

Meanwhile, the other primeval deities were continuing to bear generations of offspring, whose characteristics would give shape to the world of humankind.

The Children of Night

Primordial Night, the Dark Goddess, daughter of Chaos, shares a house with her bright daughter, Day. Their house is situated below the Earth, between the gloomy prison of Tartarus and the great halls of Hades, Lord of the Underworld, where the souls of dead mortals go to dwell.

Mother and daughter are never both in their house at any one time but greet each other on the great bronze threshold as they complete their respective circuits of the world, Night carrying in her arms the babe sleep, while Day carries blazing light.

Without taking a lover, Night brought forth numerous offspring, representative of the darker aspects of mortal existence.

Chief among the children of Night are Death and Sleep, *Thanatos* and *Hypnos*, and from Sleep comes the tribe of Dreams.

The goddess Night also brought forth the three Fates: Clotho, Lachesis and Atropos who appear in the form of three old women, intent on the task of spinning.

Clotho the Spinner spins out the thread of each man and woman's life on the day that they are born. Lachesis measures the thread with her distaff, allotting a different span of life to each mortal, while feared Atropos, whose name means the one who cannot be turned back, diminutive in stature, sits ready with her shears to snip the thread of each mortal life at the appointed time.

To each mortal, the Fates give portions of both good and evil in their life, unevenly distributed. It has been suggested by the tragedians that even Zeus himself is subject to the rulings of the Fates, and thus the three old women, bent over their handiwork, are effectively the supreme power governing the universe.

Night also brought forth Nemesis, the dread winged Goddess who punishes mortals for presumptuous and overbearing acts, catching up with them, often in unexpected and unpleasant ways, long after they believe they have escaped justice for their unlawful deeds. The plot of many Greek tragedies often hangs upon the hero or heroine being overtaken by Nemesis when disaster strikes from an unexpected angle as the result of a wrong perpetrated. Sophocles' famous play about the downfall of King Oedipus is a perfect example of this.

Hesiod tells us that Night's other children include Deceit, Friendship, and Age, along with Blame and Woe. Her daughter Eris (Strife) also brought forth a great brood of troublesome children to afflict humanity.

Night also gave birth to the Hesperides, the three sister goddesses who guard the famous golden apples that grow in the gardens somewhere in the West, far beyond the Ocean.

The Descendants of Gaia and Pontos

Pontos, the primordial Sea, meanwhile, joined with his mother Gaia and fathered five children. Their three sons were named Nereos, Thaumas, and Phorkys. The two daughters of their union were called Ceto, a sea monster, and Eurybia, of whom Hesiod only tells us that she was flint-hearted.

Pontos' eldest son Nereos married Doris, daughter of Ocean, and together they had fifty daughters known as the Nereids, sea nymphs who live among the waves. Most notable among the Nereids are Amphitrite and Thetis, of whom we shall hear again.

Dwelling beneath the sea with his wife and his many daughters, Nereos, a wise, kindly and prophetic old man, rides a hippocamp, a horse with the tail of a fish. He is known as The Old Man of the Sea.

Thaumas, the second son, married Electra, a daughter of Ocean, and they had three winged daughters: Iris, Aëllo and Okypetes.

Iris and the Harpies

Iris became the Messenger of the Gods, whose appearance is heralded to mortals by the sight of the rainbow bridge by which she travels from Olympus to the world of mortals.

The other two daughters, Aëllo, the Storm Swift and Okypetes, the Swift Flier are winged Harpies, part woman and part bird, representative of stormy winds. These harpies were later to be the tormentors of the cursed King Phineus, keeping him in a state of perpetual hunger by snatching and despoiling any meal he tried to eat. He was finally relieved of this torment by Jason and the Argonauts, who drove them off with the help of the sons of the North Wind. Their sister Iris intervened to ensure that the Harpies would not be harmed as they were chased away.

The union of Ceto and her brother Phorcys produced children who tended to the monstrous and misfortunate including the Graiae, the Gorgons and Echidna.

The Graiae and the Gorgons

The two Graiae, or Grey Ones, Pemphredo and Enyo, were women born with their hair already grey. Later writers add a third sister Deino, and tell us that the three Graiae lived by the seashore and shared but one eye and one tooth between them, which they passed back and forth as needed.

The Gorgons were three sisters who lived beyond the Ocean, close by the Garden of the Hesperides. These three women had snakes coiling from their head in the place of hair, great boars' tusks growing from their jaws, hands made of bronze and golden wings on which they flew. All three were so terrible that people turned to stone at the mere sight of them. The sisters' names were Sthenno, Euryale and Medusa. Of these, the first two were immortal, while unhappy Medusa, alone of her sisters, was subject to age and death. Medusa would eventually be slain by the hero Perseus.

Echidna and her Children

In the depths of a cave, Ceto went on to give birth to the monstrous Echidna. From the waist upwards, Echidna had the appearance of a beautiful nymph, but her lower half was that of a huge, speckled serpent. An eater of raw flesh, Echidna made her lonely home in a subterranean cave beneath a hollow rock, far from human or divine habitation.

Later, Echidna would take as her lover the serpentine giant Typhoeus. Her children include Cerberus, the many-headed hound who guards the gates of the Underworld and the Hydra of Lerna, also many-headed and serpentine in form.

One of the strangest of Echidna's children is the fire-breathing Chimaera, a three-headed beast whose body was composed incongruously of the parts of a lion, a goat and a deadly serpent.

Echidna also brought forth the ferocious and riddling Sphinx, half woman and half lion, who would one day terrorise the city of Thebes until outwitted by King Oedipus.

Another leonine child, the fearsome Nemean Lion, would one day fall to the mighty hero Herakles, who would wear his pelt in triumph.

Through her children, the serpentine Echidna thus provided generations of Greek heroes with 'monsters' against whom they could try their mettle.

Ceto's youngest child with Phorkys was the great serpent Ladon, who guards the Golden Apples of the Hesperides.

Eventually, Ceto herself would be slain by the hero Perseus as he came to the rescue of Princess Andromeda whom Ceto had been about to devour.

The Union of Okeanos and Tethys

The Titan Okeanos, meanwhile married his sister, the marine goddess Tethys. Together, they brought forth many great rivers as their sons, including; Nile of Egypt, Alphaeus of the Peloponnese and Meander whose river is known for its winding course. They were also parents to a great many daughters, three thousand nymphs known as the Oceanids These include Calypso, Doris, Europa, Eurynome and Tyche, but the most eminent of them all is the River Styx.

Unusual as a female river, Styx makes her gloomy home in Tartarus. Through her foresight, she later won special honours for herself and her children by siding with Zeus in his war against the Titans. The River Styx is the subject of the most binding oath a god may swear. If any god should break such an oath, the penalties are as severe as can be imagined against beings whose lives are endless and usually blissfully consequence-free.

For one whole year, the god lies still and helpless as if dead then, for a further nine years, they remain in dismal exile from the company of their fellow divinities and unable to partake of nectar and ambrosia, the food that sustains their divine strength and beauty. I don't believe there is an example in mythology of a god actually breaking an oath by the River Styx.

The Celestial Children of Theia and Hyperion: Helios, Eos and Selene

Theia and Hyperion, celestial gods themselves, had the

distinction of being the parents of the light-bringers of the

Heavens: Helios, the Sun and his two sisters; Selene, the

Moon and Eos, the Dawn.

Helios

Helios travels across the sky from east to west each day in his fiery chariot, bringing light to the world. His horses are named Pyroïs, Eoüs, Aethon and Phlegon. As he journeys above the earth by day, Helios is witness to all that happens in the world below.

By night, Helios travels in a cup across the Ocean, back to the east to begin a new day. Helios' wife is Rhode, a daughter of Poseidon and personification of the Island of Rhodes, where Helios had a cult site.

It is said that Helios later fathered a son, Phaeton, by a mortal woman named Clymene.

Selene

Selene sets out in her own chariot as night falls and crosses the sky, lending her own light to the darkness. Selene is best known for her love-affair with the beautiful youth Endymion, son of Zeus and a nymph called Calyce.

When Zeus asked his son what he most wished for, Endymion chose to sleep forever, remaining young and beautiful rather than face ageing and death. He now lies sleeping in a cave on Mount Latmos in Caria, in what is now Turkey. It is said that Selene visits him in his cave during the dark of the moon. This story inspired the beautiful poem *Endymion* by John Keats.

Eos

At the close of night, Eos, wearing a flame-coloured robe, takes over the skies, riding out in her own chariot drawn by her two horses named Lampas and Phaethon.

Because Eos once angered Aphrodite by sleeping with Aphrodite's own lover Ares, God of War, Aphrodite cursed her with an incurable tendency to fall passionately in love with mortal men. Among the Dawn's amorous conquests is the giant Orion, and the unfortunate Tithonios.

Eos had petitioned Zeus to grant her lover immortality but had neglected to specify that this should be accompanied by everlasting youth. Year by year, Tithonios aged, weakening and wasting away, until he was little more than a desiccated husk, a shrill-voiced cicada in the Goddess' chambers. Finally, Eos shut the feeble old man up in a room and forgot about him.

With her husband Asterios, Eos became the mother of the Winds: Zephyrus, the West Wind, Boreas the North Wind, and Notos the South Wind.

The Descendants of Phoebe and Koios

Phoebe and Koios brought into the world two daughters, Leto and Asteria. Leto, the dark-robed, gentle and kindly Goddess would one day become the mother of the twin Olympian Gods Apollo and Artemis.

Asteria married the Titan Perses and the couple had one child, a daughter, Hekate. A starry goddess, as her name suggests, Asteria was later pursued by Olympian Zeus. She turned herself into a quail to avoid him, while he chased her through the skies in the form of an eagle. Eventually, the desperate goddess plunged into the sea, where she became the Island of Delos.

Hekate was to remain a powerful and honoured goddess even after the downfall of the Titan dynasty. Hesiod describes Hekate as a benevolent and revered divinity. Zeus would give her a share in the rule of Earth, Heaven and the Underworld and she would prove friend and adviser to mortals from kings to herdsmen. She was especially associated with the protection of cities, taking the title *Hekate Propyleia* "before the gate" and is often represented with keys.

In later centuries, however, Hekate acquired a darker reputation as mistress of magic and patron of witches, with writers such as the Roman poet Horace delighting in grotesque portrayals of her cult and its depraved female devotees.

In late pagan times, Hekate was represented in the Chaldean Oracles as a cosmic goddess with power over the whole universe, building on the ancient tradition of her ruling on Earth, Heaven and the Underworld.

Hekate is often portrayed accompanied by dogs and bearing torches and is associated with the moon and with crossroads. Hekate is also linked with Artemis, Selene and Persephone and is sometimes represented in triple form. It was this imagery that was to inspire poet Robert Graves' idea of the Triple Goddess, Maiden, Mother and Crone that was to have such a key influence on the development of the Wiccan Religion.

Kronos and Rheia and the Birth of the Olympians

The marriage of the new ruler Kronos and his sister Rheia was to result in a revolutionary change to the cosmic order.

Rheia bore five splendid children; three daughters called Hestia, Demeter and Hera, and two sons, Hades and Poseidon.

Kronos, however, remembered the prophecy spoken by his parents Ouranos and Gaia, that the time would come when he would be overthrown by one of his own children, just as he had destroyed his father. In an effort to avert his fate, Kronos began swallowing each of his children as fast as Rheia could give birth to them.

Unsurprisingly, Rheia revolted against this devouring of her infants by their father. In desperation, she turned to her parents, asking what she could do to stop this destruction of her children. In accordance with their advice, when her last son Zeus was born, Rheia resignedly handed her husband a large stone wrapped in swaddling bands like a babe. Not imagining that his wife could deceive him, Kronos gulped down the stone without further investigation.

The infant Zeus, meanwhile, was being carried through the night by his grandmother Gaia, who hid him in a cave on Mount Aegeum or Mount Ida, on the Island of Crete. There he was brought up by two kindly nymphs Adrasteia and Ida and was suckled by a nanny goat called Amaltheia. Meanwhile the Kouretes, armoured warriors, performed a clashing martial dance with their shields to muffle the sound of the baby's cries.

When he had grown to vigorous manhood, Zeus returned to confront his father. Gaia, or perhaps Metis, tricked Kronos into vomiting up alive and unharmed his five brothers and sisters along with the deceptive stone. Zeus later placed the stone at Delphi as a reminder to all of his triumph. It was called the Omphalos or navel stone and was said to be the centre of the Earth.

War Between the Titans and the Olympians

Zeus and his siblings, the children of Kronos and Rheia, now made their home on Mount Olympus, establishing themselves as a rival dynasty of gods to the older generation of Kronos and the Titans. There followed a bitter and inconclusive ten-year war with the older generation of gods, who held their base on lofty Mount Othrys.

Eventually, on the advice of Gaia, Zeus brought the fruitless struggle to a climax by breaking out his Hundred-Handed uncles, Cottos, Briareos and Gyes from their long imprisonment in the bowels of the earth, killing their dragoness gaoler Campe in the process. Despite their entombment being the original pretext for Kronos' revolt against Ouranos, it seems the Hekatonchaires had been imprisoned once again by Kronos to languish in the depths of Tartarus.

After restoring them with draughts of nectar and delicious ambrosia to eat, Zeus addressed the Hundred-Handed brothers.

"Listen to me now, bright children of Gaia and Ouranos. For many years, we the children of Kronos, have been at war with the Titans, fighting day after day with neither side gaining the victory. But now, come and fight on our side with your great might and strength, remembering that we are the ones who saved you from your long and wretched imprisonment under the earth."

Cottos answered Zeus with these words. "Lordly Son of Kronos, we Hundred-Handed Ones know well that what you say is true. We know too that you are of unsurpassed wisdom and the great defender of the Immortals. It was you who brought us back out of the gloom and our cruel bonds when we had given up hope of ever being freed. We are resolved to join you and fight with you in your great struggle against the Titans."

When the Olympians heard this declaration, they burst into applause and prepared to re-enter the fray against the Titans with new heart and courage. Battle-lines were drawn up and fierce fighting broke out that day between the two sides.

So fearful was the battle as the Hundred-Handed brothers hurled great boulders from each of their hands at the arrayed forces of the Titans that the Earth, Sea and Heaven itself shook and resounded with the impact. Mighty Olympus was rocked to its foundations as the Gods charged in their fury and, far beneath the Earth, Tartarus itself trembled under the reverberation.

Now Zeus himself, full of might and fury, came hurtling down from the heights of Mount Olympus in a blaze of light, brandishing the lightning bolt and hurling thunder and lightning as he came.

Conflagration spread in Zeus' wake. The great woods caught afire and the oceans and rivers gave off mighty clouds of steam as the Earth burned, engulfing the Titans.

Seared by the blaze of Zeus' lightening, and bombarded by the three hundred boulders hurled by the mighty Hundred-Handed Ones, the Titans were utterly defeated.

In triumph, the Hundred-Handed Ones took their revenge on their erstwhile captors, imprisoning the defeated Titans in Tartarus, as far below the earth as Heaven is from Earth. Just as it would take a bronze anvil dropped from Heaven nine days and nine nights to fall down to Earth, so it would take the same amount of time to fall from Earth to the depths of Tartarus.

There, surrounded by a high wall and locked behind the bronze gates set up by Poseidon to contain them, languish the Titans in their endless imprisonment. Cottos, Briareos and Gyes chose to return to the place of their own gloomy captivity in order to guard them for eternity.

Having secured supremacy over the Heavens, the Earth and the Underworld, the triumphant dwellers upon Mount Olympus began to consolidate their rule by apportioning responsibilities.

The three brothers: Hades, Poseidon and Zeus the youngest, drew lots to establish who should rule over each of the three divisions of Underworld, Sea and Sky.

Zeus won supremacy over the sky, as well as being acknowledged king over all the Olympians and lesser beings, mortal and immortal. Poseidon became ruler of the sea, while Hades was apportioned the dark realms of the Underworld. The Earth was the common responsibility of all, subject to the authority of Zeus.

Zeus King of the Olympians

As Sky God, Zeus is represented by the high-soaring and majestic eagle. From above he controls the weather, giving or withholding rain and wielding the thunderbolt and lightning flash forged for him by the Cyclopes in their great smithy under the earth. His sanctuaries and temples are often high mountain peaks. Embodying the awesome and mysterious might of the storm, with arbitrary and destructive lightening strikes, Zeus epitomises fearful strength and power.

Zeus is traditionally portrayed as a bearded man in the prime of life, powerfully built with a lordly bearing. He is the archetypal patriarch, father of his large family and king of the gods and the earth beneath. Often, he is portrayed by Greco-Roman writers as a rather brutal and arbitrary tyrant, brooking no dissent and ready to deal out violent retribution against any challenges to his authority, whether from his own wife, Hera or from the Titan Prometheus, advocating on behalf of humanity. In Homer's Iliad, Zeus' relationship with his wife and his authority over his Olympian family is represented in rather stark terms.

In the first book of the epic, Zeus is persuaded by the nymph Thetis to allow the Trojans to prevail over the Greeks for a time in their war because her son, the hero Achilles, was dishonoured in a quarrel by the Greek leader, Agamemnon, King of Argos.

Zeus initially hesitates to grant Thetis' request, reluctant to awaken the anger of his wife, for whom Argos was a favourite city. This hesitation suggests that the power is not all on one side. However, when Hera suspiciously enquires into the nature of her husband's conversation with Thetis, Zeus threatens her with physical violence, causing her to fearfully sit down in silence. Hera's son Hephaistos then speaks up, advising his mother not to defy Zeus as he will not be able to protect her from the consequences if she does so. The last time Hephaistos tried to come between them, Zeus picked him up by his foot and threw him down from Mount Olympus.

In the course of arguing her case for why Zeus should help her and her son, Thetis alludes to a past occasion in which Hera in alliance with Athene and Poseidon were roused to open rebellion against the sovereignty of Zeus. Their plot to bind him was foiled by the swift intervention of the sea nymph Thetis, who enlisted the formidable help of Hundred Handed Briareus who came and stood guard over the king of Olympus so that no one ventured to attack him. It was perhaps in response to this event that Zeus hung his wife into outer space by her wrists entrapped in two golden bands while anvils were hung from her feet. The rest of the Olympians looked on in dismay at their queen's plight but did not dare to intervene.

Zeus is, however, very much concerned with the proper administration of justice and with the rule of kings. Oath-breaking and violation of the laws of hospitality on the part of mortals are liable to arouse his wrath.

While the final battle with the Titans established him as ruler of the universe, Zeus remained under the shadow of his predecessors, Ouranos and Kronos, both overthrown by their children in turn. The threat of usurpation never leaves the king of the gods and goes some way to explaining the ferocity of his response to possible challenges to his authority.

Meanwhile, with Kronos and Titans firmly vanquished, Zeus was able to turn his attention to the sexual pursuit of women both mortal and divine and the begetting of numerous progeny. These are portrayed as consistent preoccupations for Zeus throughout Greek mythology.

Divine Daughters of Zeus

The newly triumphant Zeus embarked on a series of liaisons with a succession of Titan and Olympian goddess, bearing a succession of remarkable daughters from these unions. These daughters of powerful divinities did not threaten Zeus' supremacy in the same way that male offspring potentially could do.

The Birth of Athene

The first woman whom Zeus courted was the Titan Goddess Metis, one of the many daughters of Tethys and Oceanos. The name Metis means Wit or Intelligence and Metis was the wisest of all beings, divine or mortal.

Unwilling in the face of Zeus' amorous advances, no doubt her foreknowledge telling her that no good could come to her of the union, Metis attempted to evade the God, metamorphosing into one shape after another. Despite this, Zeus overcame her resistance and impregnated her.

Zeus was then warned by his grandmother Gaia that a son born of union between him and Metis was destined to be the most powerful of gods and would overthrow Zeus and reign in his place, just as he had unseated his own father from the throne.

Naturally wishing to avert this fate, Zeus persuaded Metis to approach him, then suddenly opened his jaws wide like a snake and swallowed her whole. Zeus thus disposed of a future rival in exactly the same way that his father Kronos had attempted and failed to dispose of him. It was said that Metis continued to serve as a wise counsellor from within Zeus, so that by swallowing Metis, he had effectively absorbed her intelligence into himself.

Nine months after he had devoured Metis, Zeus became afflicted with agonising pains in the head. Hurrying to his assistance, clever Prometheus soon diagnosed his trouble. Cracking open Zeus' skull with an axe, Prometheus allowed the fully grown and already armed and helmeted Goddess Athene to burst forth from his head with a mighty shout. It is said that such was the might of the new-born Goddess that Olympus itself and the Earth below reeled at her coming forth. Zeus was delighted at having birthed so magnificent a daughter.

Athene is the Goddess of wisdom, craft, good counsel and weaving. A warrior goddess, she is yet temperate preferring stratagem, cunning and negotiation to mere brute force. She is the Patron Goddess of the City of Athens, for which position she defeated Poseidon in a popular election in which she offered the Athenians the olive tree in contrast to Poseidon's gift of a salt spring. It was said that following Athene's triumph, Athenian women were henceforth denied the right to vote as it was they who had secured the goddess' victory.

A virgin goddess, Athene would become a great friend and counsellor to several mythic heroes, in particular, Odysseus, a man of many wiles. Athene is portrayed as a tall warrior woman, equipped with helmet, spear and cloak. Her symbols include the owl and the olive tree.

The Daughters of Themis, Eurynome, and Demeter

Zeus then turned his attentions to another Titan goddess, Themis, bestower of justice and righteousness. As one might expect, their daughters were bringers of order and harmony to the world. They included: The Horae (Seasons), Eunomia (Good Government), Dike (Justice), and lovely Eirene (Peace).

Eurynome, the primordial Sea Goddess, was Zeus' next paramour. She bore him the three beautiful Charites or Graces: Aglaia (Beauty, Splendour), Euphrosyne (Merriment) and Thaleia (Festivities). These Graces were to become fitting attendants of Aphrodite.

Demeter, Goddess of the fruitfulness of the earth, and Zeus' own sister was his next lover. As a result of their union, she became the mother of Persephone, also known as Kore, the Maiden.

The Nine Muses

Zeus also had relations with a third Titan Goddess, Mnemosyne or Memory. It is said that they lay together on nine successive nights and as a result of this, Mnemosyne bore him the nine Muses, goddesses who each preside over the various arts such as music, dancing and the different branches of poetry.

Their names are;

Kalliope (Epic Poetry)

Kleio (History)

Melpomene (Tragedy)

Euterpe (Flute music),

Erato (Lyric Poetry)

Ourania (Astronomy)

Thaleia (Comedy)

Polyhymnia (Hymns and Pantomime).

Terpsichore (Lyric poetry and choral dance)

The nine Muses are said to make their home on Mount Helicon and have Apollo as their patron. Kalliope is said to be their leader. The poet Hesiod himself claimed to be inspired by a visitation from one of the divine Muses and they are traditionally invoked at the commencement of poems, a convention followed famously by the Iliad.

The Goddess Hera

After a succession of paramours and unwilling victims, Zeus finally chose his sister Hera to be his wife and queen, reigning by his side.

Having firmly rejected her youngest brother's initial attempts at seduction, the goddess was finally deceived by the appearance of a bedraggled and distressed cuckoo. Hera sheltered the bird in the folds of her dress, whereupon the cuckoo revealed himself to be her brother in disguise and then raped her. When we contemplate the cruel and ruthless acts committed by Hera later in her married life, it might be as well to remember where instinctive kindness and compassion had got her. After her violation, Hera felt she had no choice but to marry her brother.

The wedding of Zeus and Hera was a great and splendid affair, upon which Hera was presented by their Grandmother Gaia with the Golden Apples of the Hesperides as a wedding present. Their wedding night was said to have lasted three hundred years. The union between Zeus and Hera is known as the *Hieros Gamos* or Sacred Marriage.

The children of Zeus and Hera include two daughters Hebe (Youth) and Eileithyia, goddess of childbirth and a son, Ares, God of War, a fitting child of such a tempestuous marriage.

As a goddess, Hera was strongly associated with royalty, naturally enough, and also with women and marriage. She is usually portrayed as a tall and imposing woman, often with a crown and sceptre, modestly robed, a figure for respectable matrons to identify with. An important goddess in everyday Greek religion, Hera had many important cult sanctuaries and was particularly associated with the Island of Samos, and with the cities of Argos, Sparta and Mycenae.

In mythology, Hera tends to be portrayed rather negatively as she wreaks vengeance on a succession of the often-unwilling objects of Zeus' amorous interest as well as upon their offspring, as we shall see in particular in the cases of Heracles and Dionysos. She is, however, the patron and protector of the hero Jason of Argos as well as more generally of the Greek side in the Trojan War.

Hephaistos the Smith God

Angered and frustrated by her husband's habitual faithlessness, Hera sought to even things up by having a child of her own. Like her grandmother Gaia before her, Hera succeeded in becoming pregnant without recourse to male seed.

The child she gave birth to, a boy called Hephaistos, was lame in both his legs. Further provoked by what she saw as a failed attempt at asserting her independence as a creative power, Hera hurled the baby boy down from Mount Olympus. After falling through the air for many days and nights, Hephaistos landed in the sea where he was succoured by the kindly Sea Goddesses Thetis and Eurynome, who brought the child up. Hephaistos became a God of Smiths and Craftsmen, having his workshops under the Earth, where the great Cyclopes labour in his forge.

Only later was Hephaistos persuaded by the God Dionysus to return to Olympus to join his family.

According to a story that can be partially reconstructed from depictions on painted pottery, Hephaistos revenged himself against his rejecting mother Hera by sending her a present of a golden throne. When Hera sat in the throne, chains locked around her, trapping her in the chair. As Hephaistos was the only one who could undo the chains, Zeus offered Aphrodite's hand in marriage to any God who would bring Hephaistos back to Olympus. Dionysus sought Hephaistos out and suggested to him that by coming back to Olympus of his own accord, he could claim the most beautiful Goddess as his bride. Persuaded by this argument, Hephaistos returned to Olympus, freed his mother Hera from her chains and claimed Aphrodite as his wife.

Sadly, Aphrodite was not happy with the husband selected for her, but instead preferred the stalwart charms of the Warrior God Ares with whom she conducted an affair behind Hephaistos' back.

When Helios, the Sun God who sees all on his journey across the sky, told him of their affair, Hephaistos concealed his feelings at being rejected once again, and instead set to work in his smithy, making another set of chains of such super-fine threads that they were invisible even to the eye of a god. After rigging these chains around the marital bed, Hephaistos ostentatiously set off out of his house, giving the impression that he was preparing to go on a journey.

No sooner had Hephaistos crossed the threshold, when Ares appeared at the house and asked Aphrodite to go to bed with him, as he had just seen her husband leaving the vicinity. The moment the lovers were in bed together the invisible chains snaked around them, holding the guilty couple trapped fast in their embrace.

Hephaistos then returned to the house and loudly called upon the gods to come and see the disgraceful wrong that had been done him. While the goddesses stayed away from the shameful sight, the gods came crowding into the bedchamber to bear witness to the adultery. At the sight of the mighty warrior Ares lying a helpless captive of the lame craftsman, the gods gave way to ribald laughter. Eventually, Poseidon persuaded Hephaistos to let the lovers go, offering to stand as surety for Ares' payment of a fine in compensation.

It is said that Aphrodite bore Ares three children including the beautiful maiden Harmonia who was later married to the hero Cadmus of Thebes at a splendid wedding attended by all the Olympians.

Hestia Goddess of the Hearth

Hestia, despite her status as oldest child of Kronos and Rheia and sister to Zeus and Hera is a goddess about whom mythology is all but silent.

The Homeric Hymn to Aphrodite tells us that there were but three hearts who proved themselves immune to the goddess' power; the warrior virgin Athene, the huntress Artemis and the queenly maiden Hestia. The poem calls Hestia both the youngest and oldest of the children of Rheia being the first to be born and thus first to be swallowed by Kronos and so the last to be vomited forth. Hestia determined to remain always a virgin and took Zeus' hand as she swore an oath that she would accept no husband. Zeus accepted her resolution and offered her in exchange great honour as she keeps her place quietly at the hearth. Interestingly, in the brief Homeric Hymn that is dedicated to Hestia herself, the goddess is said to keep house for Apollo. Hearths could also form the central focus of a religious sanctuary.

Hestia's low profile in mythology is in contrast to her prominent place in actual Greek religious practice in which she had a central role, presiding over the family hearth. The hearth fire was of vital importance to Greek homes both literally and symbolically, being the major source of light and heat and where meals were prepared. New members of the family such as slaves or new brides were introduced by formal ceremonies at the hearth and the hearth fire was traditionally put out when the head of the family died. There would seem to be a connection between Hestia's unmoving position in the centre of the home and the lack of stories about her. She does not put herself in the way of adventure.

Poseidon Lord of the Sea

As the new Lord of the Sea, Poseidon took precedence over the primordial Titan sea divinities such as Nereus and Triton, who nonetheless remained as minor sea gods. Poseidon makes his home in an undersea palace, well equipped with stables for his magnificent horses.

As God of the Sea, Poseidon is usually portrayed equipped with helmet and a fisherman's trident and often rides in a chariot drawn by hippocamps. He is presented as a mature, bearded man with a tall, imposing figure. Poseidon is strongly associated with earthquakes, said to be caused by his slamming his great trident into the ground.

Seeking a maritime consort, Poseidon first courted the Nereid Thetis, but, like Zeus, he was discouraged by the prophecy uttered by Themis, foretelling that the son of Thetis would grow up to become more powerful than his father. Instead, Poseidon turned his attention to Thetis' sister Amphitrite.

Amphitrite, however, not welcoming his advances, fled to the Atlas Mountains. Her hiding place was discovered by Dolphin. Dolphin then acted as a go-between for Poseidon and Amphitrite and finally gained her consent to the marriage. By way of acknowledgement of his matchmaking services, Poseidon set up Dolphin's image among the constellations.

Poseidon and Amphitrite had three children; Triton, Rhode and Benthesicyme. Like Zeus, however, Poseidon remained a philanderer and had numerous relationships with mortals, nymphs and other beings, including his sister, the goddess Demeter, whom he approached in the form of a stallion after she had transformed as a mare to avoid him, and the Gorgon Medusa on whom he fathered the giant Chrysaor and Pegasus, the winged horse. He was also later said to be the father of the hero Theseus.

The Noble Titan Prometheus and the Creation of Humankind

Prometheus was a Titan, the son of Iapetus and Clymene. His brothers were Epimetheus, Menoitius and Atlas. Prometheus' name means forethought, while that of his brother Epimetheus means afterthought.

Prometheus' forethought told him that his fellow Titans would certainly be defeated by Zeus. For this reason, Prometheus endeavoured to persuade the Titans to make peace with the Olympians and avoid conflict. When he found they wouldn't listen to him, Prometheus swapped sides on his own account. While Prometheus convinced his slow-thinking brother Epimetheus to join him in this desertion, his other two brothers persisted in the war against the Olympians and paid the price. Menoitius was struck down by a thunderbolt, while Atlas was condemned to support the weight of the world on his head for eternity. Prometheus, through his sage advice and foresight in fact played an important role in Zeus' overthrow of Kronos and his final victory.

It was Prometheus who created the first human beings from clay. Seeing that humans lacked the swiftness, strength, tough hide or sharp teeth and claws that enabled other animals to survive, Prometheus, taking pity on their naked and helpless condition, gifted men and women with intelligence and the capacity to learn and invent. Then he began to teach his new creation the skills and knowledge that would enable them to survive and flourish.

First, Prometheus taught humans to build their own houses, instead of sheltering in dark caves. He went on to instruct them in astronomy, so that people could keep track of the seasons by watching the stars and thus know the best times of the year to sail or to plough. Knowledge of agriculture and the taming of animals, sailing, mathematics, medicine, metallurgy and the use of letters were all the gifts of Prometheus to humankind.

Prometheus' sympathy for humanity and determination to better their condition was to extend even to the point of going against the will of Zeus and this was to result in terrible suffering for the Titan.

Realising that the first human beings were allowing themselves to go hungry while offering up whole beasts in sacrifice to the immortal Gods, Prometheus devised a trick to secure a more equitable distribution for the future.

Slaying an ox in sacrifice, Prometheus divided the carcass into two heaps. He placed the bones on one side and covered them with thick fat and the hide of the animal, then he mixed the meat and entrails in a second unappetising-looking heap with the ox's stomach covering it.

Prometheus then asked Zeus which of the two portions he would accept as a fitting offering. Though Hesiod asserts that Zeus saw through Prometheus' ruse, the God nonetheless selected the apparently more generous heap, with its layers of rich fat, only to discover there was nothing but bones underneath, and that all the good meat was hidden in the other portion. From then on, mortals were able to offer the Gods the fragrant smoke from the burning of fat and bones at their sacrificial feasts while keeping all the good meat for themselves.

Angered by this trick, Zeus resolved to punish mortals for their presumption. He denied humanity the use of fire, keeping its source hidden on Mount Olympus. With no fire to cook their meat, mortals would soon learn their humble place in the great scheme of things.

Prometheus, however, was not content for his people to languish in ignorance and hardship. Defying the King of the Gods, he stole hot ashes from Mount Olympus, concealing them inside a fennel stalk. Bringing them back to the world of mortals, Prometheus taught humankind how to kindle, control and maintain fire for themselves.

When night fell, Zeus looking down from the heights of Mount Olympus, saw the flickering fires from human settlements lighting up the countryside. The God's fury knew no bounds. Having but recently established his supremacy as ruler of the Gods, Zeus could not allow his authority to be challenged in this way, and especially not by a descendant of the Titans.

Zeus ordered that Prometheus be taken to the high and desolate Caucasus Mountains, far to the north east of Greece. Here, Prometheus was to be fettered to a rock on a high mountain crag with a spike thrust through his middle, riveting him in place. Each day, an eagle, the bird of Zeus, would devour his liver, only for the organ to replenish itself overnight.

For many long centuries Prometheus suffered this unremitting torture. Finally, he was freed by the hero Herakles, son of Zeus, who, with Zeus' agreement, shot the tormenting eagle with his bow.

Pandora

Still angry that Prometheus had shared the secret of fire with mankind, Zeus decided to make the life of human race full of sorrows and hardship.

According to Hesiod, Zeus ordered Hephaistos the Smith God to create a beautiful maiden out of clay, giving her human strength and voice. Athene taught her the arts of spinning and weaving, Aphrodite gave her grace and the power of evoking desire, while Hermes gave her speech and a mind that was shameless and adept in deceit. The maiden was called Pandora, meaning 'All Gifts' a double-edged name referring both to the gifts bestowed upon her by the Gods and the jar or box she carried which was filled with all manner of diseases and sorrows which afflict humankind.

Hermes brought Pandora to Prometheus' brother, Epimetheus, who, forgetting his brother's warning not to accept any gift coming from Zeus, took the woman as his bride. Pandora then opened her jar and unleashed sicknesses and troubles without number upon men, who so far had apparently lived in contentment in a world without women. Only Hope remained in the bottom of the jar, to beguile humankind into persevering with the hard and uncertain business of mortal existence.

The Five Ages of Man

The idea that human existence has degenerated in stages from a distant and once-idyllic Golden Age is an important one in Greco-Roman culture.

When the Gods first created humankind in the age of Kronos, they made them free from toil and sorrow.

The first humans feasted merrily upon the fruits of the earth, yielded without need for ploughing, sowing or harvesting. These first people lived to a great age in the full vigour of the prime of life, not suffering the deterioration of old age. When they finally died, it was as though they simply fell into a peaceful sleep.

When this first Golden Age of humankind came to an end, the spirits of these good people remained on earth as kindly guardians of the countryside, invisible observers of just and unjust deeds, benefactors of later generations of humanity.

The second, Silver Age of humanity brought into being by the Olympian Gods was very different. The men and women of this Silver Age spent their first hundred years of life at home with their mothers in a state of childlike dependence. When they finally attained maturity, their remaining life was short and miserable. These people were too stupid and quarrelsome to thrive. They wronged each other and had no sense of the reverence they owed the Olympian Gods, offering them no worship or sacrifice. Eventually, Zeus lost patience and did away with this ineffectual second generation of humanity, whose spirits became honoured denizens of the Underworld.

The third generation of humankind brought in the Age of Bronze. This generation loved war and violence and were cruel and fierce. They wore bronze armour and lived in bronze houses and knew nothing of iron. They did not know how to make bread. These people were so warlike that they simply wiped each other out and their souls descended to the Underworld.

The fourth generation of human beings created by Zeus was the semi-divine race of heroes, those who fought at the Gates of Thebes or in the Trojan War. Some of them found an eternal home at the ends of the earth, on the Islands of the Blessed, ruled over by the exiled God Kronos.

The fifth generation is the one that exists today, a race of iron, who knows no respite from toil and from death. There remains, however, some good mixed in with all the evils that beset our current human condition.

Hesiod tells, however, of a dark time when the Iron Age too shall pass away, when babes are born with grey already on their temples, and all fair dealing and decency is lost between parent and child, brother and brother, comrade and comrade. Nemesis and Aidos (roughly Justice and Shame) in their white robes will desert the Earth and retreat to the world of the Gods. The rule of might will take over from justice and there will be nothing but violence, envy and wickedness amongst humankind until Zeus puts an end to them. Hesiod does not say who if anyone, may come after this age.

The Roman poet Virgil, writing several centuries later, brings a more optimistic perspective to Hesiod's gloomy account of humanity's suffering, decline and degeneracy. The *Georgics* is a quartet of poems celebrating farming and the land, in conscious response to the tradition begun by Hesiod with his *Works and Days*. Virgil, however, portrays the change from a life of ease to one of toil and hardship as a positive thing rather than a cause for mourning. By making life hard, Zeus forced humanity to develop ingenuity and self-reliance as they learned how to cultivate the land and domesticate animals instead of remaining in a state of childlike ignorance and dependency.

The Hounding of Leto and the Birth of Artemis and Apollo

Despite his passionate relationship with the queenly Hera, Zeus did not cease from his philandering ways. He soon took as paramour the gentle Titan Goddess Leto.

When Hera learned that Leto was pregnant with his offspring, she hounded the luckless Titaness through all the cities of the Greek mainland and the islands including Crete, Athens, Aegina, Euboia, Samos, Lesbos, Chios, and Cos. Not one of these places, no matter how wealthy or powerful, dared to give the pregnant Goddess succour or shelter for fear of the wrath of Hera.

Eventually, Leto reached the small and rocky Island of Delos. Exhausted, she bargained with the little island, promising that if she was allowed to give birth here, she would see that Delos was honoured with a great temple to Apollo, the son she was about to bear. Such a tiny, barren island, the Goddess pointed out, could hope for no other claim to fame. On receiving her oath that Apollo would not reject the island as too small and insignificant, Delos gladly agreed to shelter her and there, bracing herself for support against a palm tree, Leto prepared to give birth.

Even now, however, poor Leto had little respite from the wrath of Hera. Though she was attended by many august Goddesses: Dione, Rheia, Icheia, Themis and Amphitrite, Leto suffered the pangs of labour for nine long days. Hera had kept her daughter, Eileithyia Goddess of Childbirth shut in the palace with her, so that she could not assist the birth of her hated rival. Eventually, the Goddesses sent Iris, the winged messenger of the Gods, on a delicate mission. She was to go to Olympus, seek out Eileithyia and take her aside from Hera, to persuade her to come to Leto's help. The Goddesses gave Iris a magnificent necklace strung with golden threads to offer Eileithyia as an added inducement.

Iris flew off, swift as the wind, and soon reached Olympus. Finding an opportune moment, Iris stood in the doorway of the great hall and discreetly beckoned Eileithyia to her. When she had explained the reason for her mission, Eileithyia's heart was filled with compassion for Leto, and the two Goddesses flew off, as shy and discreet as turtle doves avoiding a hawk.

As soon as Eileitheia set foot on Delos, Leto's labour began in earnest, and she soon brought forth a girl child, Artemis, who then immediately assisted her mother in giving birth to the radiant Apollo.

Even now, Leto's troubles were not yet at an end. Unrelenting, Hera compelled Leto to resume her terrified flight from her vengeance, now with twin babes at the breast. In the course of her desperate wanderings, Leto came to Lycia, in Asia Minor. The hot sun beat down upon the exiled Goddess as she made her weary way through the fields.

It was with much joy that Leto espied a great pool of fresh water in the midst of a marshy meadow. Hurrying to the edge of the pool, she sank to her knees and was about to drink. She was prevented by the rough cries of a group of locals who begrudged the young mother a drink from their pool. Leto answered them with gentleness and courtesy; she was weary and wanted only to drink from the pool to quench her great thirst. Surely, they would have the kindness to allow her that? To recall the men to a sense of humanity, she even showed them her two babies. This pathetic gesture was in vain; the cruel louts began to jeer and threaten the friendless woman and then jumped into the pool and danced about so as to stir up the mud from the bottom and make the water undrinkable.

Leto had had enough. Remembering that she was a goddess and not the bereft mortal woman she appeared, the Titaness got to her feet, raised her arms and pronounced her doom on her tormentors. "Since you love to play about in that pool, may you remain there, frolicking forever!"

No sooner had she spoken when the cruel and ignorant countrymen found themselves all changed into frogs and they remained so ever after leaping about in their pool, still jeering with their uncouth voices.

The twins both grew up to be great and sometimes merciless archers, their arrows bringing sickness and death as well as healing.

Apollo

Apollo grew up to be the god of prophecy, of healing and of the arts, especially music. He became regarded as patron of the nine Muses of Mount Helicon.

An archer god but not notably a hunter, Apollo, known as the 'far-shooter', has a darker aspect; his arrows can bring death from plague and sickness. This happens famously in the first book of the Iliad when Apollo brings plague upon the Greek camp in anger at King Agamemnon's disrespect for a Trojan priest of the God, whose daughter had been captured. At a time when the causes of disease were little understood, an outbreak of plague could well resemble seeing individuals being picked off one by one by an invisible archer. This is the reverse side of the God's role as healer.

Apollo's patronage of healing was to some extent taken over by his son Asclepios, God of Physicians. Asclepios was the son of a mortal woman, Koronis, whom Apollo slew for her infidelity, and then snatched her unborn child from her funeral pyre. The boy grew up to be renowned as a healer of divine skill until he went too far, bringing a patient back from the dead. Alarmed at this challenge to the rule of inevitable human mortality, Zeus struck Asclepios down with a lightening bolt, much to Apollo's grief and fury, but he was later raised as a god.

Apollo presides over the great temple at Delphi, where people came to ask questions of the riddling prophetess. The site of the Delphic sanctuary was originally home to a great female serpent named Python, whom Apollo slew before instituting his own oracular temple. The Oracle of Delphi was famed in both myth and history, visited by the greatest kings and heroes seeking an answer from the god in times of confusion. The inspired prophetess would utter riddling pronouncements in response to the enquirer which would then be interpreted by priests.

Apollo is usually depicted as a handsome, beardless young man with flowing locks, casually draped in a tunic. He wears a laurel wreath in his hair and often carries a lyre. Apollo later became associated with Helios as Sun god.

Apollo took many lovers, both male and female, and fathered a number of children including Asclepios, Ion, the ancestor of the Ionians, and Aristaeus a minor deity presiding over beekeeping, but he never took a wife. Apollo embodies the ideal of youth, forever a beautiful young man on the cusp of maturity.

Artemis

As a little girl, Artemis petitioned her father Zeus to allow her to forego marriage and remain a virgin forever, hunting in the forest with her band of maidens. Zeus readily agreed, proud of his assertive daughter.

Artemis then chose a number of nymphs, daughters of Oceanos and Tethys, to be her companions, though she would later be joined by many other young women who loved the freedom of the mountains and forests. Wanting suitable weapons, the little girl, accompanied by her new companions, marched into the forge of the Cyclopes and, amidst the scorching heat and deafening crashes that made the other girls shrink back in fear, Artemis demanded of the one-eyed giants that they make for her what she needed.

Artemis is usually portrayed as an adolescent girl wearing a knee-length tunic and carrying a bow. Her hair is often bound in a simple knot at the back of her head. She is frequently accompanied by dogs, a feature she shares with Hekate with whom she is sometimes associated. She is also often depicted accompanied by a tame fawn. Artemis is also sometimes identified with Selene as a lunar goddess, corresponding to her twin brother's association with Helios.

Artemis became a protector of young girls, babies and young animals. She is particularly associated with young women around the time they get married. Despite her virginity, Artemis is also called upon by women in childbirth, taking on the role of Eileithyia. Like her twin brother, the bow that she carries indicates the power of the goddess to bring sudden death from afar. With the high maternal mortality rate in ancient Greece, making the transition from girlhood to married womanhood could be a deadly enterprise.

The Birth of the God Hermes

Maia was a shy nymph who led a retiring life in a remote cave. This, however, did not prevent her from coming to the attention of the all-seeing eye of Zeus, who came to visit her in her cave by night while Hera slept, unknowing. In the fullness of time, on the fourth day of the month, Maia gave birth to a baby boy.

Baby Hermes' precocity gave clear indication of his divine birth and his own remarkable nature. A short while after he had been born and placed in his cradle in his mother's cave, Hermes grew bored, climbed out of his cradle and left the cave.

Crossing the threshold, Hermes discovered a tortoise peacefully cropping the grass in the courtyard. At the sight of the creature, Hermes was inspired by thoughts of how it could be exploited in the furtherance of human ingenuity and art. Carrying it back into his cave, Hermes butchered the unfortunate tortoise and, by cutting lengths of reeds, strips of ox-hide and strings of sheep-gut, Hermes fashioned the shell into the first lyre.

Tuning the instrument, the new-born Hermes began to sing to himself in the solitude of the cave. He sang of his mother Maia and Zeus, telling the story of their love affair and the details of his own begetting of which he seemingly had perfect recall. Hermes went on to describe the nymphs who waited upon his mother and the great metal tripods that lay about in the cave, representing his mother's wealth.

Soon, however, Hermes grew bored of his solitary singing and set off out of the cave once again on his original errand, to satisfy his urge to taste meat.

The sun was setting when Hermes came to the mountains of Pieria, where the cattle of the Gods grazed peacefully. With supreme confidence, the infant rustler separated off fifty head of cattle from the herd belonging to his brother Apollo and drew them away.

In order to cover his tracks, Hermes somehow managed to draw the cattle along backwards so that anyone tracking their hoof-prints would imagine that they were heading in the opposite direction. He then invented the first pair of sandals, binding together tamarisk and myrtle twigs with their leaves still attached and placing them on his tiny feet to further cover his tracks.

Despite all his cunning, Hermes ran into an old countryman, tending his vineyard, who observed him leading away the sacred cattle. Stopping and addressing the old man, Hermes suggested to him that his vineyard would continue to flower and prosper if he were wise and did not speak about things he had seen which did not concern him.

Through the night, Hermes drove the cattle onwards, through mountain passes, deep gorges and fields of flowers. By dawn, Hermes and the cattle reached a meadow beside the River Alphaeus. There, Hermes fed and watered his stolen cattle, then sat down and started a fire, devising the first ever fire-stick from a laurel branch. Dragging over two of the cattle with his great and precocious strength, Hermes slew and butchered them. He then divided the meat and fat into twelve portions which he arranged on the spread-out hides on a great flat stone. Hungry though he was, Hermes took none of the meat but only drank in the delicious savour, in the manner of a god who needed no mortal food but welcomed the tribute of sacrificial offerings. Hermes then concealed the evidence of what he had done and stole back through the dawn.

Reaching his mother's cave, Hermes slipped through the keyhole and back into his crib where he lay innocently under the covers like any new-born babe, though clutching his new lyre under the blankets. Clever as he was, Hermes was not cunning enough to deceive his own mother, Maia. She berated him, asking where he'd been all night and predicting that soon he would either be led away in bonds by his wronged brother Apollo or else be condemned to the lonely and precarious life of a robber and fugitive on the mountainside.

Unabashed by his mother's scolding, Hermes reminded her that he was no ordinary baby. He had big plans for them both, he assured her. They shouldn't be lurking in obscurity in a cave but should take their rightful place in the company of the Olympians. He would be Prince of Thieves, and if Apollo didn't like it, Hermes would go to his temple at Delphi and loot the place.

Apollo, meanwhile, was out searching for his lost cattle and had just met up with an old countryman, tending his vineyard and was asking him whether he had seen them.

Heedless of Hermes' words, the old man mentioned that he had indeed seen the marvel of a baby dragging fifty head of cattle backwards along the road. The sight of a bird soaring in the sky acted as omen for the God of Prophecy and Apollo realised he was dealing with a son of Zeus. Following the backwards tracks of the cattle, he marvelled at the child's ingenuity but was still more confounded by the strange prints left by the thief that resembled those of neither man nor beast, for no one had ever before seen the tracks left by footwear, rather than a bare human sole.

Nonetheless, Apollo made his way to Cyllene, where Maia's cave was situated. When Hermes heard Apollo enter the cave, he made himself as small and baby-like as possible in his crib, burrowing under the covers. Unmoved, Apollo approached the crib and demanded that Hermes return his cattle or else he would cast him into the darkness of Tartarus.

Hermes replied by asking how he could possibly imagine that a baby only born yesterday could have stolen his cattle and told Apollo that the gods would laugh him out of court if he made such an accusation. Nonetheless, if Apollo insisted, he would swear an oath that he had never touched his cattle.

Remarking that he had the air and assurance of a hardened robber, Apollo lifted the baby up and prepared to carry him to justice. Hermes produced a loud and unexpected fart, causing Apollo to drop him in surprise.

Despite all his ruses and protestations, Apollo eventually got Hermes out of the door and carried him up to the heights of Mount Olympus, where a court had been assembled with Zeus as judge to hear the case.

Seeing his son Apollo approach with a baby in custody, Zeus raised his eyebrows and asked what grave matter Apollo was bringing to the divine assembly.

Immediately, Apollo launched into an indignant rendition of how he had been robbed by this audacious infant who had then boldly denied his crimes to his face.

The moment Apollo had exhausted his eloquence and sat down, Hermes jumped up and, pointing his finger in his celestial father's face, began protesting his innocence in terms of the utmost outrage and indignation, his eyes always darting furtively from side to side as he spoke.

The King of the Gods was amused and impressed by his young son's audacity in lying to the face of Zeus himself. After allowing the two boys to wrangle back and forth for some time, however, he decided it was time for things to be set to rights between his two children. Zeus bade Hermes show Apollo where he had hidden his cattle, inclining his head as he spoke, to indicate that this was an unshakable expression of the divine will.

At once, Hermes obeyed him and led Apollo to the bank of the Alphaeus, where the cattle were hidden. At the sight of his stolen cattle, Apollo was once again seized with rage and alarm that a baby could have perpetrated this robbery against him.

Grabbing some flexible twigs of willow that grew by the water's edge, Apollo twisted them in his hands to make a cord to bind his brother. Each time he tried to fasten the withies around Hermes, however, the twigs refused to hold him but twisted on to the ground, and began growing rapidly where they fell, until they concealed the stolen cattle from the sight of the astonished Apollo.

Wanting now to placate his angry elder brother, Hermes finally brought forth what he had been concealing under his swaddling bands the whole time – the lyre he had made of tortoiseshell.

When he handed it to Apollo, the young God was entranced. Balancing the instrument on his left arm, he plucked at each of the strings and laughed aloud with joy at the divine sounds.

Taking the lyre from him, Hermes played upon it and sang a song of the Gods and the Earth, beginning with an invocation to Memnosyne and the Muses for he was under their inspiration. He sang of each of the Gods in turn, from the eldest to the youngest, ending with his own tale.

When he had finished, Apollo commented that the song was easily equal in price to fifty head of cattle and so they were quits. He would see Hermes and his mother held in honour and would establish Hermes as one of the pre-eminent Gods with glorious gifts. Apollo went on to question Hermes all about the mystery of the lyre, wistfully remarking that it stirred his soul in a way no other music ever had.

Hermes promptly made Apollo a gift of the lyre, saying that he was worthy of that instrument of grace and eloquence. He would happily leave lyre-playing to Apollo and concern himself with herds of cattle, bringing them fertility and increase. Happily, Apollo handed Hermes his herdsman's whip and the two boys directed the cattle home before turning their own steps to Mount Olympus.

Zeus was delighted to learn that his sons had made up their quarrel and ratified Apollo's promises to Hermes, establishing him furthermore as messenger of Hades and lord over birds of omen, lions, boars, dogs, flocks and herds. Thus, Hermes took his place amongst the Olympians.

Hades Lord of the Underworld

Hades, the brother of Zeus, made his home in a palace under the earth as king of the gloomy lands of the dead in accordance with the lot apportioned to him. Hades is also ironically known as Ploutos, meaning rich, as he takes possession of all things in the end. A mature, bearded man of sombre appearance, Hades is also equipped with his famous helmet of invisibility, gifted to him by the Cyclopes.

The Greeks mostly imagined the Underworld as a place where the dead persist in a shadowy half-life as insubstantial ghosts.

The Land of the Dead

In Book 11 of the *Odyssey* there is a detailed description of the hero Odysseus' visit to the Land of the Dead.

With the help of the witch-goddess Circe, the hero reaches the kingdom of Hades by sailing to the very ends of the earth, where it is encircled by Okeanos' streams. Here Odysseus pours libations of milk and honey into a trench, offering prayers to the dead along with promises of more substantial offerings if they do his will. He then sacrifices a ram and an ewe, causing their blood also to pour into the trench. At this, the spirits of the dead begin to muster eerily, so that even Odysseus is filled with terror at the sight.

Among those the hero recognises is his own mother, but she seems not to know who he is or be able to speak to him. It is only when Odysseus allows her to drink the blood that she regains rationality and emotion. Odysseus tries to embrace his mother, but she is insubstantial like smoke. This bleak picture of the dead is confirmed when Odysseus meets up with his old comrades from the Trojan War including the young warrior Achilles who once chose a short and glorious life over a long but obscure existence. Achilles impatiently brushes aside Odysseus' compliments with the remark that he would prefer to be slave to a poor tenant farmer, living a life of drudgery than be king in the land of the dead. The only thing of interest and comfort to Achilles and the other dead is news from the world of the living. Achilles is consoled somewhat when Odysseus gives him a glowing report of his young son Neoptolemus.

While the heroes of Troy and the heroines of old are permitted to wander the fields of Asphodel with gloomy dignity and Orion the mighty hunter busies himself pursuing the ghosts of the beasts he killed in life, certain of the dead are less fortunate. We see King Minos of Crete, son of Zeus, acting as judge to the dead. Later writers add his brothers Rhadymantys and Aeacus as judges of the Underworld. Odysseus' attention is then drawn to certain individuals who had sufficiently offended the Gods to be judged deserving of perpetual torment. Sisyphus is doomed to push a great boulder up a hill only for it to turn and roll down to the bottom each time. Tantalus stands in a pool of clear water which vanishes as soon as he stoops to drink from it, while succulent fruits dangle above his head only for the branches to jerk up above his reach. Tityrus, who once tried to abduct the Goddess Leto, has his liver gnawed night and day by two vultures. It seems to be indicated that quite an exceptional level of transgression such as direct insult to the Gods was required to incur such a sentence rather than the usual run of human misdeeds.

Other writers such as Hesiod and Aristophanes also tell us that in order to enter the realm of Hades, the dead must cross the River Styx in a boat steered by the grim ferryman deity Charon. Bodies were customarily buried with a coin to pay Charon and it was believed that the souls of those whose bodies were denied proper burial would not be able to find rest in the Land of the Dead but would wander as forlorn and restless ghosts until the required rites were performed.

The entrance to the Underworld is guarded by Cerberus, the monstrous three-headed hound of hell. Hesiod remarks drily that the dog is very friendly to those going in but rather less so to those who try to leave.

The bleak picture of the mindless, gloomy existence of the dead was alleviated by the growth in mystery cults such as the Eleusinian Mysteries and the Orphic sect which taught that their initiates would be granted special access to a joyful afterlife. As time went on, beliefs about the afterlife became more varied and complex with, for example, the growth of belief in reincarnation.

The Rape of Persephone and the Anger of Demeter

As a goddess, Demeter enjoys an unusual freedom, being neither a perpetual virgin like Athene, Artemis or Hestia, nor bound in marriage like Hera or Aphrodite (however irregularly in the latter case). This unregulated sexuality may be related to her position as goddess of agricultural fertility. Her boundless fecundity on which humanity and animals depend upon for life cannot be subject to control. The second part of her name is linked to the word for mother. As well as bearing a daughter Persephone by Zeus, Demeter is also said to have lain with Iasion in a thrice-ploughed field in Crete and given birth to a son, Plutos, meaning wealth. Zeus soon after slew Iasion with a thunderbolt for his temerity at lying with a goddess. Another of Demeter's children is Iacchus,

Persephone, Demeter's daughter by Zeus, grew up into a beautiful young girl. She is also known by the name Kore, simply meaning The Girl. Her beauty was such that in time she came to the attention of her Uncle Hades, King of the Underworld. Desiring her as his bride, he approached his brother and Persephone's father, Zeus to ask for her hand in marriage. Zeus discreetly gave his permission without consulting with Persephone's mother Demeter.

The girl herself, meanwhile, was happily playing with her friends in a grassy meadow, picking the beautiful flowers that grew there. Suddenly, the ground gaped open before Persephone and from that yawning chasm rushed Hades, King of the Dead in his chariot. Seizing the terrified girl, he plunged back with her under the earth and into darkness.

Persephone cried out desperately for help, calling on her father, the King of the Gods himself to save her. Zeus, however, had placed himself conveniently out of the way and was at one of his temples, receiving offerings from mortals. The only deities to witness her abduction were Helios the Sun God, who sees all, and the kindly Goddess Hekate who heard her cry out.

As Persephone was drawn down into the infernal darkness, Demeter caught the tail-end of her despairing cry. Realising that someone had abducted her, Demeter tore the veil that covered her head, flung off her dark cloak and went flying like a bird over land and sea in search of her beloved daughter.

For nine days, Demeter wandered over the earth, bearing a torch in each hand, searching and asking everyone she met whether god or mortal if they had seen her daughter. All those she asked were either unable to tell her what had happened, or else unwilling for fear of the wrath of Hades. In all that time, Demeter did not refresh herself with ambrosia or nectar nor washed her body with water.

On the morning of the tenth day, Demeter was met by the Goddess Hekate. Hekate confirmed that she had heard Persephone being abducted but had not been able to see who it was who took her. Together, the two goddesses approached Helios the Sun God and stood before the horses of his chariot.

Demeter asked Helios, if he had any regard for her, to tell her truthfully what he had witnessed, for he sees all things that happen on earth, below his soaring chariot.

Helios responded to Demeter's request, and told her what he had seen. He then counselled Demeter to come to terms with what had happened: Hades was not a bad match for her daughter, being ruler over all the dead as well as Demeter and Zeus' own brother. With that, Helios called to his horses and they resumed their course across the sky.

So far from taking Helios' advice, Demeter was overcome by grief at the loss of her daughter and fury at Zeus for having connived at her abduction behind her back. Shunning the company of the Gods, Demeter changed her form and entered the world of mortals.

In her guise of an old woman, Demeter came to the town of Eleusis, near Athens. Reaching a shady spot by a well, she sat down and rested out of the sun. Presently, the four young daughters of King Celeus: Callidice, Cleisidice, Demo and Callithoe came to the well to draw water. Seeing an old woman sitting there alone, they addressed her kindly and asked her who she was and why she sat alone and did not enter the town where she would be welcomed.

Demeter told the girls that her name was Doso, and that she came from Crete, having been captured by pirates who brought her to the mainland where she had succeeded in escaping them, and had been wandering ever since. She asked the girls if they knew of any house where she could earn her living as nurse, or servant or housekeeper.

In response, Callidice told the old woman that her mother had just given birth to her only son, a late child, and she was sure her mother would be very thankful to have a competent nurse to rear him. At Demeter's nod of assent, the four girls filled their pitchers and hurried home to ask their mother if she would receive the old woman.

Hearing their account, Queen Metanaira asked her daughters to hurry back and tell the old woman she was hired. The girls ran back to find her, and escorted Demeter back to their home. While the girls raced ahead, Demeter trudged behind, gloomy in her dark cloak, her face veiled.

Metaneira was sitting by a pillar in her great hall with her son in her arms. When Demeter crossed the threshold, it seemed for a moment that her head reached the lintel and the doorway shimmered with a strange radiance. Filled with sudden awe, Metaneira got to her feet and asked the old woman to sit on a brightly draped couch. Demeter, however, refused the luxurious seat and remained standing silently, until a servant woman Iambe set out a simple jointed stool and placed a sheepskin over it. There Demeter consented to sit, wrapped in grief for her abducted daughter, keeping her face veiled, not taking any food or drink. Resourceful Iambe was having none of this, however. With a volley of obscene jokes and gestures, she finally provoked the distraught Goddess into smiling and laughing. Demeter then accepted a drink of mint and barley, refusing wine.

As nurse to Demophoon, Metaneira's little boy, Demeter anointed him with ambrosia, the food of the Gods and breathed upon him with her divine breath, causing him to grow rapidly and seem more like a divine being himself than an ordinary baby. Curious as to the secret of Demeter's remarkable effect on her baby son, Metaneira decided to spy on her one night.

From her hidden vantage point, Metaneira observed the nurse dangling her beloved son into the fire. Naturally, Metaneira cried out in fear and horror.

At her cry, Demeter turned upon Metaneira, her eyes blazing with anger, casting the unfortunate infant to the floor in disgust as she did so.

"Stupid mortals! You never understand when something is for your own good! If you had let me finish, I would have burned away the mortal part of your son and made him as a god, but now he will be mortal and subject to death."

Demeter then cast off her disguise as the old woman Doso and appeared before Metaneira in all her glory and beauty as a Goddess, so that a wonderful fragrance wafted from her robes, while a bright light filled the house. Demeter then commanded that a temple be built for her at Eleusis, outside the palace. This was done the next day.

Sitting in her new temple, Demeter continued to brood with grief and rage on her stolen daughter Persephone. That year, none of the seed sown in the ploughed fields would germinate and no crops grew. Humankind was in danger of starvation and, consequently, the Gods were in danger of losing the worship and offerings that humans provided. This caught Zeus' attention. Hastily, he sent Iris, messenger of the Gods, to tell Demeter to come to Olympus and cease from her disastrous withdrawal from the world. Demeter did not respond to Iris' entreaty. In turn, Zeus sent one God after another to intercede with Demeter, offering her all manner of gifts, but she was obdurate, swearing she would not return to Olympus or allow the crops to grow until she was reunited with her daughter.

Eventually, Zeus gave in; he called to Hermes, telling him to descend to the Underworld and get Hades to give Persephone back.

Descending to the Underworld, Hermes delivered the unwelcome message to the King of the Dead, whom he found with his unwilling Queen sitting beside him. Concealing his feelings, Hades expressed his acceptance of Zeus' command and told Persephone she could go home to her mother. Secretly, however, Hades forced her to swallow a few pomegranate seeds, the only food she had taken in his house.

Making ready his chariot, Hades conveyed Persephone and Hermes back up through the earth until they arrived at Demeter's temple. When Demeter and her daughter saw each other, they ran to embrace joyously. As she held her daughter, however, Demeter sensed that something was wrong. She asked Persephone if she had taken any food in the House of the Dead. Persephone confessed that she had been forced to swallow the pomegranate seeds. Regretfully, Demeter told her daughter that this meant Hades still had some claim upon her, and Persephone would have to spend part of the year with Hades and the rest of the year above ground reunited with her mother.

Demeter and her daughter then returned to Olympus and feasted with the rest of the Gods and fertility was restored to the Earth.

Herakles from mortal to God

The creation of humankind opened an exciting new avenue for the exercise of Zeus' libido: mortal women. While many of the resulting children of these liaisons grew up to be great heroes and founders of mortal dynasties, two, Herakles and Dionysus, achieved divinity and a place for themselves on Mount Olympus.

Herakles was born to Alkmene, a princess of the great city of Mycenae. While Alkmene's husband Amphitryon was away at war, Zeus, who was taken by her charms, came to her in the guise of her husband, and thus engendered in her the baby Herakles, destined to be the greatest Greek hero of all. The following night, when the real Amphitryon returned, a second child, Iphikles, Herakles' mortal twin was conceived.

Hera, of course, was furious when she learned of Alkmene's pregnancy by Zeus. By what seems a strange irony, Herakles' name means Glory of Hera, though the Goddess dogged and bedevilled his life from beginning to end. From one perspective, however, it was through overcoming the trials he was set by Hera that Herakles won his way to glory.

Hera's campaign against Herakles began when he was still in the womb; she saw to it that his cousin Eurystheus was born before he was and thus inherited the throne of Mycenae instead of him.

After his birth, Hera sent giant serpents to the cradle Herakles shared with his twin brother Iphikles. The baby hero strangled the two snakes with his bare hands and was found laughing to himself while Iphikles whimpered in fear.

Hera's darkest act against Herakles, however, was to afflict him with madness, causing him to murder his wife Megara and his three sons. It was to purify himself of this crime that Herakles undertook his famous Twelve Labours under the direction of his cousin King Eurystheus by way of atonement.

Having won fame for his mighty deeds, Herakles was finally brought low when his wife Deianira, hoping to regain his affections, smeared what she thought was a love potion on his tunic. It turned out to be a poison which ate away agonisingly at the hero's flesh. Desperate to end this torment, Herakles had himself burned on a great pyre and was translated to Olympus to live as a demi-god. He was then married to Zeus and Hera's daughter Hebe, Goddess of Youth.

The Birth of the God Dionysus

Dionysus was the son of Semele, daughter of King Cadmus of Thebes. Zeus had been visiting the young princess in secret in her chamber. When Hera discovered her husband's affair, she came up with a plan to destroy her mortal rival.

Taking on the guise of Semele's old nurse Beroe, Hera approached the girl, who told her joyfully that Zeus himself was visiting her in her bedchamber each night. Hera asked Semele how she could be so sure. It would not be the first time that a mortal man had tricked a simple girl into bed by claiming to be a god. There was only one way Semele could be sure she was not being lied to. The next time her lover came to visit her, she must extract from him an oath to fulfil whatever she wished; then she must demand that he appear to her in all his divine glory as he would appear to Hera herself in their bedchamber. The innocent Semele agreed to take her wise old nurse's advice.

The next time Zeus came to her, Semele asked him to swear to grant whatever she wished. Once Zeus had nodded his head in assent, an irrevocable expression of the divine will, Semele demanded that he appear to her in his full divine splendour.

Aghast, Zeus tried to stop her from uttering the fatal words, but once they had been spoken, he had no choice but to keep his oath. Sorrowfully, Zeus retreated to Mount Olympus, where he equipped himself with lightning and thunderbolt before descending back to Earth in his chariot. Zeus entered Semele's bedchamber in a blinding flash of light and heat and Semele was consumed by the flames. At the last moment, Zeus snatched up the child Semele carried within her and sewed him up within his thigh, nurturing him until he was ready to be born.

Brought up secretly on Mount Nysa, young Dionysus grew into a handsome, rather androgynous, young man with flowing locks. His tutor was a Satyr, a lustful, rustic demi-deity, half-man and half-goat called Silenus, a round-bellied drunkard who accompanied him on all his adventures.

Early on, Dionysus discovered the secret of wine-making. Bearing the thyrsus, a wand tipped with an acorn and garlanded with ivy, Dionysus and his band of followers travelled the world, even as far as India, spreading the knowledge of the potent vine and turning the world upside down.

Everywhere, women left their homes and went to join Dionysus in the woods and mountains beyond the city, dancing ecstatically. Where he was opposed or ignored, Dionysus' wrath could be terrible and destructive.

Angry Hera afflicted him with madness, but Dionysus, journeying through Syria and Egypt, met with the Great Goddess Cybele, who healed and purified him.

Eventually, Dionysus descended to the Underworld, where he redeemed his mother Semele and brought her to Olympus, where she took the name Thyone and the divine status of both were acknowledged.

Dionysus is the patron God of tragedy, and the Greek tragic performances were sacred occasions, held in his honour.

Pan the Shepherd God

Pan is generally agreed to be the son of Hermes, but there are a number of different stories about the identity of his mother. The Homeric Hymn to Pan tells us that once Hermes worked for a time as a shepherd in the service of King Dryopes in Arcadia in order to win the hand of the king's daughter, who is known as Dryope after her father. When, in due course, a child was born of their union, the midwife was so shocked by the baby's strange appearance that she ran away. Pan was born with goat legs and the budding horns of a goat upon his head and was a noisy, laughing baby. Noting the fearful response to his son in the world of mortals, Hermes scooped up the infant, wrapped in hare skins, and brought him up to

Mount Olympus, where the gods welcomed him with gladness. Dionysus, who had been brought up by the goat-legged satyr Silenus, greeted him with especial joy.

Other stories say that the mother of Pan was Oinoe (Wine), Penelope, the wife of Odysseus, or even Amaltheia the nanny goat who nurtured the infant Zeus.

As the half-wild god of shepherds and goatherds, Pan especially haunts deserted places deep in the woods and the countryside where he plays upon his shepherd's pipes or syrinx. Syrinx was originally a nymph who fled his sexual advances and at her desperate prayer was turned into a reed in order to escape him, only to be fashioned into an instrument for his use. Pan is also known to cause sudden *panic* to seize the hearts of travellers if they trespass on his grounds at noontide.

According to an eerie anecdote from Plutarch, a discursive essayist and biographer of the 2nd century CE, Pan is the only Greek god to have actually died. He tells the story of an Egyptian sea captain named Thamas who was sailing one night past the Island of Paxi when he heard a strange voice from the island calling him by name three times. When he finally ventured to respond, the voice instructed him to wait until he reached the mainland and then to cry out in a loud voice, 'Great Pan is dead!' The captain did as he was told and from the mainland came great weeping and lamentation in response from a multitude of voices.

Gigantomachy: The Revolt of the Giants

The defeat of the Titans had left Zeus and his brothers and sisters as victorious rulers of Earth, Sea and Heaven. The Olympians were not, however, allowed to enjoy their supremacy unchallenged for long.

Gaia, angered by the defeat and banishment of her Titan offspring at the hands of her upstart grandson, in time brought forth a race of Giants, terrifying in their size and strength. Their appearance was made the more fearful by the thick manes of hair that hung down over their shoulders. Their feet were covered in dragon's scales.

The mightiest of the Giants were Porphyrion and Alcyoneus. Alcyoneus could not be killed in battle, as long as he was fighting on his native land of Pallene. These Giants now laid siege to the Gods, hurling great rocks and burning oak trees at their home on Mount Olympus.

There was a prophecy that the only way the Giants could be defeated by the Olympian Gods was if they had a mortal as their ally. Knowing of a certain herb that would make the Giants invulnerable even if these conditions were met, Gaia hurried out in search of this wondrous plant.

In order to circumvent her, Zeus showed his might by ordering Eos, Selene and Helios not to shine forth in their chariots, keeping the world in darkness. Groping about in the gloom, Zeus himself found the herb which he plucked and hid. Zeus then sent out the Goddess Athene to secure the mighty hero Herakles as their mortal ally.

A terrible battle was then joined between Gods and Giants. In accordance with the prophecy, only Herakles could strike a mortal blow against the Giants, so the Gods sought to wound each Giant and then call Herakles over to deliver the killing blow.

At first, Herakles tried shooting Alcyoneus with arrows, but, of course, as soon as he touched his native land of Pallene, his wounds were healed and he leapt up even stronger than before, renewed by the contact with his native soil. Finally, Athene advised Herakles to drag the Giant beyond the boundaries of his native land. Once Alcyoneus was outside the territory of Pallene, Herakles was able to dispatch him.

Mighty Porphyrion confronted Herakles and Hera together. As Porphyrion attempted to rape Hera, Zeus struck him down with a thunderbolt and Herakles took the opportunity to finish him off with his bow.

Another Giant, Ephialtes, was shot in the left eye by the Archer-God Apollo, and then was shot in his right eye by Herakles.

Even the less obviously warlike and heroic of the Gods had their part to play in this fight for survival against their towering enemies.

The Giant Eurytos was struck down by the handsome Wine God Dionysus with his thrysus, his ritual wand, entwined in ivy.

Hekate, the Titan Goddess who had wisely sided with the Olympians, used her ritual torches to slay the Giant Clytios.

Hephaistos, the lame Smith God used slingshot of red hot iron from his forge to bring down the Giant Mimas.

Hermes the Trickster used the Helmet of Hades to become an invisible assailant and brought down the Giant Hippolytus.

The Fates, three elderly women usually bent over their wool work, slew two Giants, Agrios and Thoon with bronze cudgels.

Meanwhile, the Warrior Goddess Athene slammed the Island of Sicily down on the Giant Encelados as he fled from her. Ruthlessly pragmatic, Athene skinned another of her gigantic victims, Pallas, and used his thick hide as body armour.

Poseidon chased the giant Polybotes out to sea before breaking off a fragment of the Island of Cos and crushing him under it. That fragment became the Island of Nisyron.

Artemis killed the Giant Gration, and the remainder of the Giants were blasted by Zeus' thunderbolts and then shot by Herakles as they lay in their death throes. Once again, the Olympian Gods triumphed against their enemies and reigned supreme.

Typhoeus and the Last Battle

Angered still further by the defeat of the Giants, Gaia now joined in love with Tartarus and brought forth her last and most terrible child, Typhoeus.

Typhoeus' head scraped the very stars. One hundred additional serpentine heads sprouted from his shoulders. Each of these snake heads spoke in a different voice. While they could speak in a language intelligible to the Gods, the heads could also bellow like a bull, roar like a lion or, weirdly, bark like puppies. When the serpents hissed, the noise resounded off the mountains to terrifying effect. Typhoeus' legs were also of serpentine form, while his body was covered in wings, and bright fire flashed from his eyes.

This terrifying being set himself against the Gods of Olympus.

While Hesiod assures us that Zeus overcame Typhoeus with the might of his thunderbolt after a terrific battle, a very different and less flattering version of events is preserved for us in Apollodorus of Alexandria's *Library of Greek Myth*.

Apollodorus tells us that at the very sight of Typhoeus laying siege to Olympus, hissing and screeching and hurling burning brands, the Olympian Gods all fled in confusion to Egypt.

When Typhoeus pursued them, the Olympian gods and goddesses all concealed themselves in the guise of various animals. This story may be connected with the Greek attempt to rationalise the Egyptian custom of worshipping their Gods in animal form.

 As Typhoeus approached, Zeus attempted to hold him back with a volley of thunderbolts, but Typhoeus kept coming. Once he was in range, Zeus attacked him with an adamantine sickle and chased him to Mount Casion in Syria.

Typhoeus was badly wounded, and Zeus was confident that he would be able to overcome him. Typhoeus, however, entangled the limbs of the God in his serpentine coils and wrested the sickle from him. He then cut out the tendons of Zeus' hands and feet, rendering him helpless and immobile, and bore the Ruler of the Gods on his shoulders across the sea to a cave in Corcyra, where he left him, along with his severed tendons, concealed in a bearskin. Guarding the wounded God, day and night, was Delphyne, who was half maiden and half serpent.

Vigilant as she was, the Dragoness was not clever enough to defeat Hermes, Prince of Thieves. Accompanied by Goat-Footed Pan, Hermes was able to steal into the cave and restore Zeus' tendons to him.

Restored to his full strength, Zeus returned to Mount Olympus, only to come tearing down from the sky on a chariot drawn by winged steeds, sending Typhoeus running for his life before a volley of furious thunderbolts.

Typhoeus fled to Mount Nysa, where he encountered the three Fates. The Fates offered Typhoeus mysterious fruits which they promised would make him immortal. Gratefully, Typhoeus partook of these, not realising that he had been tricked and instead the fruits had sealed his doom.

Zeus now caught up with Typhoeus and pursued him as far as Thrace, to Mount Haemus, where they recommenced their terrible combat. Mighty Typhoeus tore up whole mountains to hurl at Zeus, but the Sky God used his thunderbolts to deflect them back on him. It is said that the streams of blood that poured from Typhoeus as he fought gave Mount Haemus its name, for the meaning of Haemus is 'bloody'.

Finally, Typhoeus fled to the Island of Sicily, where Zeus slammed great Mount Etna down on top of him, crushing him forever. The volcanic eruptions of that mountain are said to be Zeus' still smoking thunderbolts.

From then onwards, Zeus and the divine race of the Olympians ruled unchallenged.

Deucalion and Pyrrha and the Great Flood

The story of how the Gods decided to wipe out the human race in a great deluge goes back to the mythology of ancient Mesopotamia.

The Babylonian *Atrahasis Epic*, dating back to over a thousand years before the first literature of Greece, recounts how the Gods first created humankind to be their servants, and then, finding them to be too noisy and tiresome, decide to drown them. One mortal, Atrahasis, is warned by the wise god Enki to build and provision a great boat and thus survives the flood. The gods then become reconciled to humanity's existence. This story seems to be at the root of both the famous biblical account of Noah's flood and of the various local flood myths that are alluded to here and there in Greek mythology. The Roman poet Ovid provides the fullest and most vivid account of the myth in Greco-Roman literature.

Ovid's account of the Great Flood is positioned after the coming of the Iron Age, so that unlike Hesiod, he imagines present humanity as belonging to an improved Fifth Age.

Deucalion was the son of Prometheus, while his wife Pyrrha was his cousin, the daughter of Epimetheus and Pandora. He and his wife were exemplary in their piety to the Gods and their upright behaviour.

The same could not be said for their fellow humans, men and women of the hard and cruel Iron Age. Zeus received report after report of ever more staggering examples of human cruelty, greed, dishonesty and depravity.

Unwilling to believe that mortals could have degenerated to such a state, Zeus decided to visit the earth in person to see for himself if things were really that bad.

Descending from Mount Olympus, Zeus wandered from place to place dressed as a mortal traveller in cloak and broad brimmed hat. For the ancient Greeks, hospitality, or *xenia*, treating strangers and travellers well, was one of the most important of the virtues, and so this disguise would give Zeus an excellent opportunity of judging how far humanity had sunk.

On all sides, Zeus came face to face with such examples of human wickedness that he concluded the reports had not gone far enough. Eventually, he came to the home of Lycaon, King of Arcadia, arriving at his palace just as night was falling. Zeus let it be known that he was a god in disguise and the ordinary people began to do him appropriate honour.

Lycaon himself, however, mocked their piety. He resolved to put the stranger's claims to a public test. Seizing hold of a man sent as hostage by the nearby tribe of Molossians, Lycaon cut his throat and butchered him like a beast, boiling and roasting different portions of the unfortunate man's flesh. Lycaon then had this meat set down before the stranger. If the stranger partook of this terrible cannibalistic feast, it would prove that he was no god and, furthermore, he would be defiled by having eaten human flesh. Lycaon then planned to murder him in his bed that night, in order to drive the lesson home.

Zeus, of course, knew immediately what had been set before him. Filled with rage that such a vile trick should be attempted upon him, he brought down the house with a thunderbolt, leaving it in ruins.

The king fled in terror into the countryside, where he found himself undergoing strange alterations in form. His clothes transformed into a shaggy hide, his arms became legs, while great pointed teeth stretched his slavering jaws. With a snarl, Lycaon turned upon the grazing flocks and worried them, taking well to his new form of the wolf.

Zeus, however, was not satisfied with this punishment of the worst offender. Profoundly shocked by all that he had seen on earth, he went back to Mount Olympus and called an extraordinary meeting of all the gods and goddesses. When all the Olympians were assembled in the marble council chamber, Zeus described to them his sojourn on earth and the depraved state of mankind he had witnessed for himself. He followed this with the pronouncement that he could see no other remedy but to destroy the human race entirely.

On hearing this, the other Olympians found themselves in something of a quandary. They dared not openly disagree with Zeus, who wasn't notably fond of his pronouncements being put to democratic debate, but at the same time they grieved for the threatened destruction of humanity. Who would leave offerings at their altars? Would the world simply be left desolate, to be overrun with wild beasts? What would happen to all the nymphs, satyrs and other semi-divine beings who lived on earth?

Guessing their unspoken concerns, Zeus reassured the assembled deities that a new, improved human race would be brought into being to repopulate the earth.

It now only remained for Zeus to decide upon the precise manner in which he would wipe out the earth's population. At first, he was resolved upon fire as a cleansing method, and was ready to blast the earth with his thunderbolts, unleashing an even greater might and fury than when he warred against the Giants. Just in time, Zeus remembered a prophecy that one day the entire universe would be destroyed by fire, including even the dwelling place of the gods. He therefore settled upon flooding the earth and drowning all the living creatures upon it.

Zeus' first step was to imprison the North Wind in the Cave of Aeolus, along with any other winds that might help to scatter the clouds. He then sent forth the South Wind, his wings and beard dripping with raindrops, his terrible face veiled in darkness.

Iris, in her dress of many colours, busily kept the low hanging clouds swollen with rain, even as the South Wind wrung the moisture from them in his great hands causing a great downpour upon every part of the Earth.

The mighty torrents of rain flattened the crops growing in the fields, destroying that year's harvest.

At this stage, Zeus called for reinforcements from his brother Poseidon. Poseidon in turn summoned all his rivers to a war council, commanding them to burst their banks and flood in full spate. The rivers gladly do as they are bid, sending all their waters rushing out of their courses, towards the sea.

Poseidon then slammed his trident down on the Earth with such force that the ground fissured, allowing the waters a way in to overrun the fields and towns. Now the great torrents of water swept away everything; crops, orchards, herds of cattle, people and even the sacred temples put up to honour the Gods.

Any house that remained standing became a place for curious sea nymphs and fish to explore, swimming from room to room. Dolphins frolicked amongst the treetops, seals basked where once goats had grazed. Meanwhile, all the land animals drowned, the birds flew overhead until they dropped from exhaustion, and the few men and women who survived the floods took refuge in boats, or on the summits of the highest mountains. Eventually, however, even they, one by one, succumbed to starvation.

Stranded on the peaks of Mount Parnassus, Deucalion and Pyrrha were the only survivors. Having been warned of the impending flood by Deucalion's father Prometheus, they had provisioned a large boat in which they had sat out the storm.

Deucalion was the most virtuous of all men living, while Pyrrha was the best and most pious of women. When Zeus saw that these two were the sole survivors of the flood, he was satisfied that his work was done. He released the North Wind from the Aeolian Cave so that he could blow the rain clouds from the sky. Zeus then called on Poseidon to send the seas and rivers running back to their proper beds.

When the Sea God Triton blew upon his conch shell, sounding the retreat, the rivers came rushing back to their proper courses; the seas respected the shores. The waters gradually retreated until land appeared, although it was now barren and strewn with algae and sand from the sea.

When Deucalion and Pyrrha looked down from the heights of Mount Parnassus and saw that they were the only survivors on this desolate Earth, they lifted up their voices and lamented.

Seeking an answer to their plight, the couple approached the temple of Themis, the Titan Goddess of law and justice, having first ritually purified themselves by sprinkling fresh water on themselves from the nearby stream. The temple was dank and discoloured with the remains of seaweed. Unable to light a fire, Deucalion and Pyrrha prostrated themselves on the temple steps and, kissing the damp stone, prayed aloud. They implored the Goddess' mercy, asking how human life was to continue when they were the only two left alive.

From the depths of the temple a voice responded. "Walk away from this temple with heads veiled and your robes ungirdled. As you go, throw behind you the bones of your mother."

There were a few moments bewildered silence while this message was absorbed and then Pyrrha, most pious of women spoke up. "I am sorry, but I could never commit such a sacrilegious act as to disturb the bones of my mother."

Together, Deucalion and Pyrrha then turned the strange message over in silence, trying to make sense of it.

Finally, Deucalion broke the silence. "I don't believe Themis would ask us to do anything so wicked as desecrate our parents' bones. By our mother, I think she means the Earth, the mother of all, and by her bones, she means these stones lying in the ground."

There seemed to be no harm in trying this idea out, so, accordingly, Deucalion and Pyrrha veiled their heads and filled the folds of their robes with stones, then, without looking behind them, they walked away from the temple, casting back the stones as they went.

As the stones landed on the ground, miraculously, they began to change, losing their hardness, growing and reshaping before the astonished eyes of the virtuous couple. All the stones that were cast by Pyrrha shaped themselves into women, while all those thrown by Deucalion assumed the forms of men. Thus, Deucalion and Pyrrha repopulated the Earth and we are the sons and daughters of stone, drawn from the bones of Mother Earth Herself, tough and built to withstand hardship.

As the sun warmed the still-saturated earth, the combination of heat and moisture engendered new growth, and Earth brought forth plants, animals, and birds so that the world was once again full of life.

BIBLIOGRAPHY

Primary Sources

Apollodorus, *The Library of Greek Mythology*, Oxford World's Classics, trans. Robin Hard, 1997.

Aeschylus, *Prometheus Bound and Other Plays, Penguin Books Ltd, trans. Phillip Vellacott, 1961.*

Hellenistic Poetry; An Anthology, selected and trans. Barbara Hughes Fowler, University of Wisconsin Press, 1990.

Hesiod, *The Homeric Hymns and Homerica*, Hesiod et al, Loeb Classical Library, trans. H. G. Evelyn White, 1936.

Homer, *The Iliad, Vols 1-2*, Loeb Classical Library, trans. A. T. Murray, 1924.

The Odyssey, Penguin Classics, trans. Robert Fagles,2006

Myths from Mesopotamia; Creation, the Flood, Gilgamesh and Others, ed. and trans, Stephanie Dailley, Penguin Books, Revised edition, 2000.

Ovid, *Metamorphoses*, Vol 1, Loeb Classical Library, trans. Frank Justus Miller, Revised G. P. Goold, 1921.

Secondary Sources

Greek Religion, Walter Burkert, Blackwell Publishing Ltd., trans. John Raffan, Oxford, 1985.

The Greek Myths, Robert Graves, Penguin Books, 1992 (A very detailed and vivid retelling, complete with invaluable references, though the copious footnotes reflect the author's own idiosyncratic views on myth and history and should be taken with a pinch of salt.)

The Oxford Dictionary of Classical Myth and Religion, ed. Simon Price and Emily Kearns, Oxford University Press, 2003

###

9 781720 109792